CAFÉ CONFESSIONAL

CAFÉ CONFESSIONAL

Stephen Roberts

AVVENTURA

Cover design by Stephen Roberts
Back cover photo credit: Ezra Jeffrey-Comeau
https://unsplash.com/@emcomeau

ISBN-13: 978-1-936936-16-8

Published by
Avventura Press
133 Handley St.
Eynon PA 18403-1305
www.avventurapress.com

POEMS

❧ **Pretending to Be Alive**

When I'm in the cafe
I'm not really here
I don't exist
I simply observe
everyone else
like i'm watching
tv
I'm not a part of society
the crowd
the group
the people
I'm just on the periphery
something you kind of
see, but not clearly
mostly ignored
out of sight
out of mind
just watching
they don't see me
and don't need me
I don't speak to them

but I need them
I need to be around
others
and pretend to be
alive
like them.

🜲 Commiserate

I look at people
hoping they will
see me
know my thoughts and
pain
and say I have that
too

❧ Solutions

It's always there
in the back of
my mind
the alcohol lets
it come to the front
and speak
encouraging me

Chess

A friend once told me
the person who cares
the least
has the most
power
in a relationship.

✿ Empath

Being empathetic
skin is an open
wound
everything gets in
nothing soothes it
you feel everything
all the time
even the things
that are not yours
to feel.

✍ **Hopeless Romantic**

Love being an
infection
that nothing can cure
a constant fever
and chills
made worse by the
contagion's presence
your immune system
cant fight shit
and every contact
from them is a
new infection.

✿ Punching Bag

I remember the cellphone
had smooth plastic
edges
the edges were rounded
but anything small can
hurt
if enough force is
behind it
especially when applied
to my face
her favorite target.

✿ Haunted Sushi

After a date
and i'm sitting
in a restaurant
we used to go to
all the time
it's familiar in
a tragic
traumatic
kind of way
I'm probably still
in shock from
the date
my embarrassment
I like her a lot
I'm hoping I
didn't screw
it up.

❧ I Hate Nostalgia

On the way there
I realized my
GPS hates me
Its joy in existence
is made sweeter
by making me
squirm
I typed in her
address
and off I
  went
only the phone
went where it thought
I wanted to go
back into the
grip of emotional
pain
I started to recognize
streets
a familiar exit
before I knew it

I was back there
her street was one
turn away
I stopped at the
red light
expecting her
to appear
as if summoned
by my fear
she never did
and I got the green
and I flipped her street
off as I drove by.

❧ Sisyphus

I'm really tired of
the unrequited
the unreciprocated
the one-sided
unending circular
mess
as if casting
my lure with
the wrong bait
only I'm the
bait
and that can't
be changed.

❧ Anxiety

I want to walk
into a room
unburdened by
anxiety
I don't want to
run to my car
gasping for
comfort.

❧ Croissant et Fromage

Im sitting in
a Japanese restaurant
the place is
empty
so I sit the
furthest down the
bar as possible
half a mile
from the waitress
I'm not a masochist
music is put on the
speaker
French bistro music
I'm confused where
I am
and what I
should feel
I eat my sushi
my mind prepping
my taste buds
for croissants and

cheese
they probably make
that roll here.

❧ Getting Older

Im at the point
in my life
where I can look
back
and reflect on
memories
long past
and wish for
the glory days.

✻ Attention

Say her name
say it a thousand
times in one
sentence
you had her
attention
you had her
patience
you burned
her out.

Fiber

Am I really at
this point in my
life where I have
my bowel movements
dictate my mood
and my life?
am I speeding
through my youth
ahead to my golden
years?

❧ **Diverticulitis**

Am I aging
the reverse of
Benjamin Button?
Is my life over
before it even
began? I'm young and
shouldn't have to deal
with this shit.
Living my life
from one moment
to the next
unsure of what
will happen to
me
what food will
hurt me
can't go anywhere
have to stay
home
eat nothing but
pureed shit

drink your breakfast
lunch and dinner.

✦ O.C.D.

I feel the
constant need to
study
inanimate objects
to notice every
single blemish,
dent, and scar.

❧ Decisions

Some days you
are pulled back
into nostalgia
you hate nostalgia
it makes you
vulnerable
to the feelings
you've been trying
to suppress
the events you
were trying to
forget
you think of
every dumbass
thing you've done
every poor decision
you've made
how you would
be better off
now if not for
that one
mistake

🕸 30

a period of
time is over
and another
begins
your 20's are
for adventure
and building
a future
your friends are
getting married
and having
children
they have
mortgages
and a steady
pay check
you have an
extra degree

live with your
parents
balding head
and diverticulosis.

✥ **Anticlimactic**

Every complication
setback
push back
set back
annoyance
blank nothingness
ended without
much ado
about
nothing.

❧ Zen

Remarkably
in public places
my mind doesn't
work
it's blank and
devoid of thoughts
Starbucks is
filled with hipsters
sipping
nursing a small
coffee and hunched
over their MacBooks
typing their latest
masterpiece
or some other
shit that requires
an audience
to be written.

The Wrong One

I keep thinking
of her
waiting
for her
I didn't text
so she would
have to show
that she cared
too
the wrong one
texts you back.

A....

You fantasize
about meeting
her
what you'd do
together
how close she will
stand next to you
you remember
that school trip
to the museum
how casually you
tried to be there
pretending to read
the exhibit plaque
She pretended to
read it too
her shoulders
touched yours
it was heaven.

❧ Café confessional

I like sitting here
because it makes
me feel ok with
existing
I'm uncomfortable
everywhere else
The creative juices
flow here
I feel free to read
and write
at home there is
guilt
and disappointment
writing is illegitimate.

Birth Control

I sit
reading my book
drinking my tea
feeling exhausted
I didn't sleep well
like most nights
A young couple
comes in
their tiny person
waddling in front
they make no
effort to quell
the noise the
child's making
outdoor voice
indoor voice
both the same
the mom doesn't
hold her back
lets her wander
up to strangers

and garble her
baby speak
the mom laughs
and knows that
everyone else thinks
this is cute just
like she does.

❊ The Next Generation

A granny talks
to her grand daughter
the kid brings
a stack
waiting for grammy's
approval
she imparts the
oldest cliched saying
"never judge a
book by its cover"
"Just like life"
she says
she said it with
the weight that
a poet would
use to show
their self-importance
their never before
heard brilliance
if that is the
best she can do

I wonder if
she's even had
an original thought.
It's probably not
her fault
society doesn't encourage
originality
it thrives on
repetition
and recycling
what once worked

❧ Buffer

It's not encouraging
seeing those
kids
they're more than
a group
they're a mob
they stare at
me
at my table
outside
they want my
table
greedy bastards
your mob of a
family
is no excuse
I need this
table more than
you
it shields me
from the likes

of you
inside i'm surrounded
and overwhelmed
trying to justify
my existence
my right to be there.

❧ Home-wrecker

I saw a face
I didn't want
to see today
or ever again
It belonged to
a criminal
the face
is covered in
psoriasis
pockmarked
with
blotches of red
why aren't you
in jail?

✿ The Past

So many things
drag me back
memories mostly
I did my
best to brush
them under the
carpet of my mind
but much like a
'mess on a carpet
the stains seep through
corrodes the integrity
of the carpet
eats it away
the only way
to save a carpet
is by properly
cleaning it
not to let the

mess sit for too
long and set in
out of site
is not out of
mind
in fact it
has the element
of surprise.

✿ If Only

Just once I want
to go to the cafe
sit down with
my tea
and be at peace
just once I
want to be
sat down, my
nose in a book
and look up
and see a
woman staring
at me.
I would look at
her and she would
notice I've seen
her,
and she would
avert her eyes
embarrassed
there would be

a second glance
from us both
and the intension
would be plain
just once
on that day
I wouldn't be
alone.

❦ **Oblivious**

I just realized
why
on the night that
I drove you
to meet him
at the dive
bars
that you told
me to leave
and eat dinner
I was worried
you were
embarrassed
of me
that I wasn't
cool enough
to hang out
but it was happening

even then
I was so trusting
and oblivious.

✤ Babcia

an elderly polish
woman.
she was my ex's
grandmother
all of my elders
have passed on
I grew up without
knowing them
So Babcia
adopted me
she fondly called
me her
Boychik
my happiest memory
of her
was sitting at her
dinner table
with the family
She was speaking
polish and I
heard a word

I said "Pochwa"
and after a
stunned look
Babcia burst
with a thunderous
laugh
her belly shook
and tears came
she asked where
I heard that word
she said it
had been a
long time since
she laughed that
hard.
Thats how I like
to remember
her.

✧ Swipe culture

I'm so tired
of looking at
duck faces
the pursed lips
selfie saying
what?
yes your lips
are glossy
you must use
chapstick everyday
what's you routine?
So many faces
and i'm charged
with judging yours.
It tells me
what kind of
person you are
If you're my
type
If we have
a future together

A picture is
supposed to say
a thousand words.
your face is
supposed to say
that and more
do you feel
guilt for swiping
left?
your not supposed
to.
it's a brutal
world
and dating is
no different.
no one knows if
you swipe left
on them
it's the easiest
rejection
and anonymous
the only rejection
is not getting

a match
not a big
deal
a lesser man
might feel the
world has rejected
him.

Morticia

All this time
spent swiping
and I can't
find my Morticia.

❧ Driving in cars alone

I remember
driving my car
for the first
time alone
in a long
time
much like coming
home to an
empty house
It felt barren
and hollow.
perhaps haunted
I turned on
the radio to
hear a voice
I never talked
much while driving
multitasking was
never my forte
my co-pilot made
up for my

silence
silence is something
you get used to
at first heavy
then
comforting.

❧ Two Way Street

Why should I
forgive you?
when I don't
afford that luxury
to myself?
Friendship is a
two way street
and you treated
it like a
one way.

✺ Moon Child

I don't know
what it is
about the evening
and early morning
hours
that holds me
in their grip
I don't want
to go to
sleep
I don't want
this to end.
I put on
a bad movie
load my pipe
and enjoy my
time of quiet
enjoyment
truly it is
the only time
I am comfortable

in my own
skin.

✥ No Escape

Social media has
ruined my sense
of self
my sense of
security
my spirit
profiles are no
longer about your
true life
but what you
want people
to see
and perceive
of you.
It's bad enough
that we pretend
to be friends
on line
why do I
need to be
shown pictures of her randomly
on my feed?

✺ Expectations

Social media presents
lives in a
perfect way
it makes you
feel as an
underachiever
nothing in your
life is done
on time
you've fallen behind
on every aspect
of life
you shall never
catch up.

❧ Stephen Who

Part of what
is so painful
is seeing how
easy it was
for you to
move on.
It was so
easy in fact
that you moved
on a year
before we separated
one can't help but feel it
a reflection on
oneself
am I that
forgetful?

❧ Extended Empathy

My powers of
self consciousness
know no bounds
watching a girl
perform with guitar
in a coffee shop
and I cant
help but be
frozen with anxiety
and self consciousness
it might as well
be me on that
stage.
I've taken empathy
to a new
level.

✤ Phone Home

I've said this
a lot
but it's always
true
I'm very much
like an alien
in public
doing a human
impersonation
i'm an alien
experiencing a
live performance
in a coffee shop
for the first
time
ordering a coffee
business as
usual
but what are
you supposed to
do when you

sit down?
when the singer
is right in
front of you?
are you supposed
to stare at
them?
it feels wrong
somehow
indecent
it feels rude
to stare when
they are doing
something so
exposed
I wouldn't want
people staring
at me if
I were performing
this coming from
the person who
can't make eye
contact.

✤ Watering Hole

It is a
human version of
the watering hole
people gather around
to rest and
quench their thirst
only the danger
is not there
no lions or
jackals will
stalk you here.
the only threat
is to look
out of place
and be stuck
on the outside.

❧ A Social Excursion

Many people go
out on these nights
for different reasons
sometimes I wait
and hope for
human contact
I'm an orphaned
loner waiting to
be adopted by
some adventurous
woman.
Maybe she would
walk up to my
table
and ask if
this seat was
taken.
her pants are
summer weight
black with white
checks

remarkably
similar to my
flannel shirt.
my shirt and
her pants
were meant to
be together
my shirt could
be perfectly
happy with her
pants
I'm sure my
shirt would tell
her it's either
both of us
or neither
we're a package
deal
but I would
not stand in
my shirt's way.

⚘ People

It's been a day
of minor
inconvenience
The grocery store
was the land
of the walking
dead
and an old
woman in an
old jalopy
almost backed into
me.
This day reminds
me that being
outside the home
means people
people in the
bookshop
I sat in the
corner
not the one

with the comfy
chair mind you
Two middle aged
perhaps older gentlemen
sat in front
of me
apparently one's leaving
a job and
reached a great
revelation about
being able to
walk away
I guess everybody
is dealing with
change at some
point
and making revelations.

The Comfy Chair

There are four
comfortable chairs
at the book
store
and they're all
by the window
They're grouped
together in twos
with a small
table in between
them
Both chairs face
each other
there is an
unspoken rule here
you never sit
across from a
stranger
so only two
of the chairs
are used at

a time
well a stranger
sat down opposite
me on the comfy
chair
this has never
happened before
and I'm stunned
what am I
to do?
what does this
mean?
for the socially
awkward?
this is hell.
do you talk?
this seems awfully
intimate
best to avoid
eye contact.

✺ Outliers

There is something
about being on
the outside
both metaphorically
and literally
it's used a lot
by directors and
artists
the director can
put the viewer
outside a window
implying simple
observation
but put the camera outside
a nice home
and the viewer
is the outsider.

✦ The Peanut Gallery

I just want
someone to
watch horror
movies with
especially the
bad ones
that you need
to make rude
comments about
to make them
bearable
and for some
reason keep watching
them.

✿ **Depression**

Depression has done
a great deal
for me
it steals who
you are.
Depression is
smiling at a
woman at the store and
when not returned
means there is
something wrong
with you.
Sometimes your not
yourself for so
long
you forget how
to be you.
It's seeing the
world through
dark lenses
depression is not

wanting to cook
your dinner
not wanting to
eat.
It is seeing
the worst in
yourself.
the light
is overshadowed.

✢ **Tolerance**

It's funny what
you can tolerate
when you become
used to something
and when you
no longer have
to tolerate it
how quickly you
forget about it
what was once
the bane of
your very existence
is no longer
in your hemisphere
of thoughts.

❧ **Stigma**

When you are
a man who
has been the
receiver of abuse,
or
assault
you're treated and
perceived
differently.
your male friends
call you pathetic
and question your
manhood
and usually say
they wouldn't
have put up
with it
told her to
beat it
or hit back
women tend

to follow two
reactions
the first begins
incredulity
disbelief
then a look
saying your not
a man.
Just like your
guy friends
then they say
they wouldn't have
put up with
it.
Maybe hit back
I say I couldn't
do that
the same look
the other reaction?
Pity.
and concern
enough to be
polite.

some tenderness
somehow you feel
like damaged goods
maybe they see
you that way
and always will
you regret saying
anything
in the end
everyone's reactions
and opinions are
just that
it's not their
life and not
their problem
it's yours.

⚡ **Perseverance**

One of the
hardest parts
of being an
undiscovered
artist
is continuing
to have hope
to continue
to produce work
without the
guarantee
that your work
will ever leave
your house
that it will
see the light
of day.

-

🏃 Hypochondria

Living the life
of a hypochondriac
is very exhausting
that sore on
your tongue might
be something else
that headache might
be something else
everything else might
be something else.
or worse.

⚘ **Halloween**

Halloween has always
been my favorite
holiday
there's something
about the leaves
on the ground
crunching under your
feet
sleepy towns
with old buildings
decorated with skeletons
and jack o' lanterns
staying out late
past your bedtime
trick or treating
there's something
magical about that
night.

✺ **Young and Old**

My usual comfy
chair is taken
I'm a young
looking old man
the cafe is busier
than usual
filled mostly with
old white men
reading gun and ammo
magazine.
the comfy chairs
are open
a young woman
and friend
snatch them up
let them have
it
the young inherit
the earth after all
and the comfy chairs.

✺ Ode to Analog

I sit in
the corner
wondering what
they're talking about
they have iced coffee
if it were fall
they would be pumpkin
spice lattes
they don't have
books
but they have
cell phones
I wonder if
they ever felt
a pen
scratching across
real paper
noticing how the
ink at first
is glossy
then slowly

soaks the page
and becomes
dull
or if they
ever filled a fountain
pen
got the ink
on their fingers
for days,
no one has
inky fingers
anymore.

☙ **Mantra**

sometimes
all you can
do
is move on
with your life
forget what was
said or done
and remember
tomorrow is a
new day.
the sun erases
the misfortune
of the previous
night.

✤ Time Travel

The long hours
of the evening
make me yearn
for the friends
I once had
I watch tv
shows from my
youth
they make me
nostalgic for a
time when imagination
was more important
even nurtured
and anything was
possible
for my future
was unknown and
unwritten.

⚘ Sadist

If you're an
introvert
prone to bouts
of depression and
self-doubt
it can be very
easy to judge
yourself harshly
that inner critic
never knows when
to be quiet
and it doesn't
like to be
silenced.
anything you do
or don't do
can be twisted
into new methods
of torture
with so many
things to choose

from
you'll have endless
hours of fun
torturing yourself.

❧ Fraud

You call yourself
a goth
You can work
in that store
with all the
dead things
wear all the
costumes you want
but I'll always
remember
that you hated
it
when I watched
the Addams Family
you fraud.

❧ To Thine Self Be True

Something important
for a woman
to remember
when dating a
man
never lose who
you are
be true to
yourself
and your nature
your blond hair
was fine
just like your
nails
you needn't put
on a costume
to suit his
ego.

❧ The Collector

A small man
is he
in stature
and in
nature
he is a
collector
of objects unusual
and
of the fairer
sex
it is no
mistake that
they are not
all dissimilar
so much so
they should dwell
in Stepford
a collector
is a
collector

his collection is
vast
and she a part
of it.

❧ Scrolling

Do you ever
spend your days
stagnant
frozen in fear
unable to reach
your well of
motivation?
a smart phone
is a terrible
distraction
sucking you
in
fooling you into
a sense of
activity
and accomplishment.

✿ uncanny

It's funny the
things that trigger
memories
and faces
a book you
read in someone's
company
a store you
pass on a
familiar street
a restaurant
you used to
like
Grandmama Adams
reminds
me of her
grandmother
mostly in looks.

🪰 Social Anxiety

I'm often told
that no one pays
any attention
to you and
your worries
your embarrassment
goes unnoticed
everyone is too
pre-occupied
with their own
problems to notice
yours
well,
I notice.
I see everything
that woman is
asleep in her chair
in a public cafe
she snores gently
That old man
sitting across

from that pretty
  woman
he's haunched over
with old age
and drops his
book
another elder sits
reading his
wild west magazine
his farts have
a blast radius
of five feet
he's not bothered.
not everyone
but some
notice everything
so
your chances are
good.

✤ Waiting Room

The book store
coffee shop
is just one
of life's waiting
rooms
with more up
to date magazines.

❧ Acceptance

In the throes
of loneliness
I fear
the eventual
decent into
spinster hood
living my days
solitary
indulging in
vices
habits and ways
set in stone
weaker moments
open the mind
to nostalgia
and regrets
did I do
the right thing
fleeing that mess?
the sound mind
says

you lost nothing
and gained
everything.

🐾 **Nirvana**

There are moments
when my mind
is light
creativity flows
and the world
is not so
dark
the catalyst is
unknown
and elusive
it's been a
life long pursuit
I live for
those moments.

✺ Take That

What was it
that the
high school guidance
counselor said?
he will never
get into college?
A mop and bucket
was in my
future?
years later a
masters degree
framed on my
wall!
saddled with crippling
student debt
interest compounding
everyday
no relief in
sight
I sure showed
her.

✤ **Waiting**

I'm waiting for
that moment
when a woman
looks at me
and appreciates
my existence.

✢ Drowning

Depression
is
drowning in
quicksand
it's not that
you don't want
to act
to do
to feel
it's that it's
very hard
you're frozen
even breathing
takes more effort.

Paternal Instincts

The mom walked
in the cafe
little kid in
tow
baby in arms
she bought a
snack for her
kid
she devours it
ravenously
the young girls
next to her
college age
look upon the
youngsters
with longing eyes
maternal instincts
seem to live
in young women
always waiting to be
needed

I admit
it was cute
when the kid
took the whole
cookie when her
mom wasn't looking
it's always cute
when it's someone
else's kid
I've never had that
paternal urge
and don't particularly
want that urge
to emerge anytime
soon.

❧ Belong

You would think
that I had gotten
used to the
solitude by now.
I have gotten
used to it
actually
by solitude
I mean the
loneliness that is
a byproduct
of it
Does anyone ever
get used to
that?
If people say
they are content
with it
they're lying
humans are social
creatures by nature

we have always
sought our tribe
to belong.

Can't Look Away

People are obsessed
with tragedy
they watch it
on the news
it plays all
day
one tragedy after
another
they can't look
away
they watch it
on the shows
they read about
it in novels.

✸ What I Care About

In the bathroom
zipping up my
fly
I noticed my belt
it was too
long
so I had
chopped off some
of its length
the end was
raw and a
light shade of
brown
clashing with the
black outer color.
I immediately thought
of what my
ex would say
"you can't go
around looking like
that, it's embarrassing."

There are things
in life that
I care about
and things I
don't.
you I don't.
the brown stays.

❧ Celebrity

Watching celebrity culture
I can't help
but wonder
what someone from
an earlier time
would make of it
imagine a peasant
sat in front of
a television and
told they could
watch a person
more well off
than them
go about their
day
spend their money
and receive special
treatment
and it plays
all day
I imagine they

would think us
crazy
both for lifting
these people above
ourselves
and paying to
watch it.

✵ Perfection

On this talk show
the host could
not get over
how good this
pop star looked
at 50 years old
they wished they
could look
so hot
did our ancestors
care about looks?
not when chasing
down a wooly
mammoth
they hunted
gathered
drank
slept
and reproduced
they knew what
was important

and what wasn't
today
we're not trying
to outrun death
in the shape
of predators
we have too
much headspace
room for nonsense
we're obsessed with
teeth!
perfect rows of
white teeth
so bleached they
look fake
imperfection has become
our new predator.

✹ Taking the Reins

It's hard to
imagine anything
different
anything better
I'm like a
horse with
blinders on
and the driver
keeps me on
the same path
any happy thought
that steers me
in a better
direction
is driven away
by his whip
I'm told to
get myself in
a better
direction
how does a

horse get himself
unsaddled?

❦ Idols

How did those
tragic painters
muster the will
to paint
when the world
was so unkind?
How did van Gogh
dredge up the
spirit
to paint hope
when his mind
constantly betrayed
him?

Jewelry

Body adornment
is a form
of self-love
it's telling yourself
you are worthy
of decoration.

✖ **Running to Bukowski**

The world became
too much
as did my life
so I ran
to Bukowski
Whenever my efforts
were met with
silence
I ran to
Bukowski
When a friend
let me down
I ran to
Bukowski
When my love
was unrequited
I ran to
Bukowski
When I felt guilt
for drinking
too much

I ran to
Bukowski
When I felt
guilty for being
alive
I ran to
Bukowski
When I feel
self-conscious
about my poetry
I run to
Bukowski.

❧ **Candy the Go Go Dancer**

One night
early years of
college
A girl we knew
who made the
rounds through my
group of friends
was performing in
a go go club
to pay for school
everyone of my friends
had seen her naked
at one point
or another
and this was
my chance
I drove,
my one friend
George
was navigator
his navigational skills

sucked as much as
his personality
he led us down
and around all over
Philadelphia
and we didn't
arrive to the
promised land till
late,
very late.
We missed her
performance
George was dead
to me from then
on.

✴ **God the cock blocker**

Denise was the
first girl I
ever fell in
love with
It was freshman
year of college
it was an
exciting time for
me
I was a very
sheltered child
and this new
city offered much
Denise was my
safety
she was outgoing
and showed me
friendship
I needed that
being away from
home was very

scary to me
we did everything
together
we were inseparable
when vacation came
I hated being apart
I wrote her letters
Our favorite spot
was the duck pond
we'd sit and talk
it was very peaceful
I remember the
night that
ruined everything
I spoke of
how much she
meant to me
and then she
spoke the phrase
I never expected
to hear
She said God
didn't want us

to be together
she needed a man
who would
teach her about
God
and lead her
to Christ
the next year
she spent in
Rome
with her new
cult of Christian
friends
I couldn't see
her anymore.

❧ Musings from the litter box

The serotonin
has left my
brain faster
than my cat
runs away
from the litter
box
and it is
just as revolting.

✠ There's No Going Back

It's a different
coffee shop today
It's in a college
campus
and it's completely
different
no oldsters
just young people
wasting time between
classes
It was a feeling
of no longer
belonging
not that I felt
unwelcome
more knowing myself
there is no going
back.

❧ It's All the Same

Grief,
sadness,
depression,
it's the same
thing as being
drunk
wasted
you reach out
to people you
haven't spoken to
in years
seek out help
from those who
don't know you
spill your guts
to deaf ears
making bad
decisions
and an ass
of yourself.

❧ No Man is an Island

No man is
an island?
I disagree
while you may
be born
into this world
surrounded
by people
aided by a
doctor
when you pass
on
no one can
do it with you
or
for you.

✤ **Glass Houses**

I lived in
a glass house
once
with tinted
windows
I could see
out
but no one could
see in
without pressing
their face against
the glass
hands cupped
around their
face
squinting
not many people
tried.

❧ **Mr. Scrooge**

Today was a
bitter December
day
a day the
cold goes right
through to your
bones
I stopped my
car at a
dilapidated gas station
reminded me of
north Philadelphia
in those places
one thought always
goes through your
mind
while exposed out
of your car
am I safe?
the people look
rough

anyone could be
measuring you up
I've never been
robbed
today, I thought,
might be the day
a rough looking
fellow called out
to me
walking closer
he said he
lost his house
and needed change
he gave up on me
when I denied
having change
it pained me
to turn him
away out of
fear
I rationalized
there are shelters
and services

and felt like
Mr. Scrooge
asking if there
were no
workhouses
no prisons
I wondered about
my life
I'm sheltered now
but what about
the future?
when my support
moves on?
are the streets
in my future?
I hope strangers
are nicer to
me
than I was to him.

❧ Return to academia

I spent many
years hating school
and the books
I didn't understand
the endless writing
the highlighters
now I find
myself
carrying around
a bag
filled with books
paper
and pens
becoming a poet
wishing I had
a highlighter
to mark a
pearl of wisdom
from Bukowski.

❧ I'm ignoring you

I've always been
a private person
but people today
they've gotten worse
human interconnectedness
has all but
slipped away
with even more
opportunities to
connect
people turn their
noses up
and move in
the opposite direction
literally turning their
backs on people
this woman takes
the chair next
to me
and turns it
around

so her back
is to me
mind you there
are two rows
of chairs
facing each other
and she chooses
to interrupt the
feng shui
and turns sideways
This place is
full of chairs
if she didn't
want to see
my ugly mug
she could have
sat across
the room behind the pillars
some people go
through a lot of
trouble to let
you know they
are ignoring you.

Aging hipster

I suppose that
you change how
you see yourself
as you get
older
somehow I still
think of myself
as a younger
man
despite the ever
growing bald spot
I wonder when
it will get
to the point
of looking ridiculous
my dangling earring
Doc Marten boots
and nose ring
perhaps never
my generation will
be the first

to have stretched
earlobes
tattoos
and nose rings
in the nursing home
what a sight
that will be.

❧ Caught in the headlights

Being in Scranton
kicks up old
forgotten memories
like one of the times
I drove to
Dallas to pick her
up from
her yet unrevealed
boyfriend's house
on the way
back
a car's headlights
were right in front
of my car
I realized
the car was
going the wrong
direction
it was headed
straight for us
I swerved into

the other lane
and the car
just missed us
her cheating almost
killed us.

❧ **Alive with misery**

There's nothing
like a health
scare
to make you
appreciate life
you even appreciate
the bad things
your thankful for
illness
because it reminds
you that you're
alive
to feel it
you appreciate
the terrible relationships
because you felt
alive with
heartache
it's better to
live in misery
than not live

at all
and not aware
of anything.

❧ The Vacuum

Facebook
has become a
vacuum
for sad thoughts
and depression
nothing is heard
it's all absorbed
and lost
in the void
you could be
drowning
and no one could
hear you.

K

a   barista
a manager
at the
Starbucks
her colored blond
hair is up
in a scrunchy
in a way
she's very much
like every other
woman in Hazleton
she's attractive
in a too old
for her age
kind of way
she has too
many cares
too many worries
she's probably
a single mother
got pregnant

by the wrong
man
she's missing teeth
either side
on the top
of her mouth
she stepped out
for a cigarette
one of few
joys she gets
in a day
she's very like
the women
of Hazleton
and yet one
of the few
that still has
dignity.

I want off

Is life
a ride
we can jump
off of
when we're
ready?

❧ **Bukowski**

His writing wasn't
hard
but he paid
his dues
through a
rough life.

✎ Social encounters

Sometimes I seek
social encounters
Starbucks is a
place to find
it
especially if you
just want to
be around other
people
without the hassle
of having
to talk to
them
sometimes
just knowing
they are there
is comfort
enough
sometimes knowing other
people still exist
is a comfort.

❧ Imagine

I imagine
the aftermath
of dragging
a razor blade
down my arm
of sending a
chunk of lead
on a tour
through my skull
it's not
remarkable
few would find
out
possibly through
the paper
maybe a Facebook
post
on my behalf
few acquaintances
from my past
would vaguely

remember me
as the quiet
guy
he always looked
pensive
serious
they're not surprised
it ended that way
they would remember
me for a
day
maybe two
and life would
move on.

✺ **Slow and steady**

I worry about
myself
my future
can I provide
for myself
in the end
nothing is certain
but
Bukowski
lived both
in poverty
and in
comfort
he didn't
gain success
until his forties
so there must
be hope for
us all
to make it
eventually.

Highlighting

The older I get
the more dog
ears appear
in my books
I started to
carry a highlighter
in my pocket
and relevant lines
are bathed in
neon
why do we
do this
why is it
worth
permanently marking
a perfect page
just because someone
wrote words in
an order that
pleased you
are they sacred

words from God?
no
do they lead
to personal wealth?
no
do they help
you at all
no
do you see
yourself in these
words?
perhaps
and not feel
so alone
yes
maybe even
understood.

✿ Life raft

she was a
life raft in
a tumultuous
sea
she showed me
friendship
comfort
consistency
unconditional hope
life had taken
on a brighter
hue
hope had the
potential to
appear again
and I had
less trouble seeing
the future in
a better way
nothing is that

easy
life's little wrinkles
aren't smoothed
over that easily
and I should
have expected a
yang to the yin
equal and opposite
reaction
as it goes
she just as
easily removed her
gifts
as she lent
them
the good mornings
and goodnights
replaced by
silence
and unfollowed through
promises
I am
a bowling pin

set up to be
knocked down
at someone else's
leisure.

✦ Lost in the woods

I feel like
I'm lost
in the woods
or a fog
can't see anything
beyond my nose
and it feels
like it's been
an eternity
or a minute
both at the
same time
I've got the
feeling
the fog could
lift
a path could
be shown out
of the woods
if I do
just one thing

and fuck if
I know what
that is
I watch films
about art and
artist's
hoping the life
will jump start
within me.

Money

it's nothing but
paper and ink
numbers on a
screen
those made up
numbers
the inked paper
causes people to
live on the
street
because they have
none
we made it up
and we keep
it alive
just believing
in it
and our belief
keep them
living in the
gutter.

❧ Everybody sleeps

I always wondered
do people in
desperate survival
situations
no longer consider
existential problems
do they no longer
worry why they
exist?
why they struggle
and just focus
on surviving
I think that
they probably
focus on those
questions just as
much
everyone has to
close their eyes
and sleep
and think sometime.

❧ Head space

Imagine killing
yourself
and ask if
that person would
be upset
what would they
do?
that will help
you figure out
if they should
be in your
life
if they are
worth thinking about
if they are
worthy of the
space
they are taking
up in your
head.

❧ Unseen scars

Life is easy
when you are
pretty
not hunkered down
with your depression
and ugly mug
some of us
have to work
hard
just to get
on the track
some of us
have to work
very hard just
to want to
live
it's an unseen
fight
no scars
no proof of
your hard work

every human life
has value
just being
born
so that's something.

❧ Frozen man

As Bukowski said
I am the
frozen man
not necessarily
unhappy
most definitely not
happy
just there
not sure where
it started
just remember being
a young child
not being interested
in much of
anything
except being a lone
with comic books
and a sketch pad
it wasn't until
adulthood I

learned the phrase
going through the
motions.

✺ **Hashtag**

The world and it's
culture is being
reduced to a
#hashtag
nothing is sadder
than seeing your
culture and life
summarized by
a social media
character.

✿ Hope

It's hard to
enjoy the present
when you don't
believe you have
a future.

❧ Disease

They say you
aren't your
disease
that life can
go on
with minor
adjustments
you aren't the
anxiety you
cause
others
you aren't the
concern they
show
you aren't the
pity they show
on their face
you aren't the
anger they
scream at
your face

you aren't the
reason they
want to leave
you
you aren't the
hate they say
you bring out
of them
you aren't the
end of their
life
you aren't the
end of
you
you aren't the
burden weighing
them down
you aren't a
choice
a symbol
a mistake
a number
or

the fault of
their problems
you are you.

❧ Wear and tear

The world is
a big factory
with every nut
and bolt doing
it's share
some are content
to be a rivet
hammered in a
hole
holding two walls
together
what of the bolts
chipped threads
that no longer
turn
no longer hold
those walls together
what of the components
that are no longer
useful?

❧ Responsibility

The power that
we give each other
over ourselves
is dangerous
we can destroy
each other's self-worth with a
single word or
phrase
our lives can
be centered around
our words to
each other and the
promises we make
and they are frequently
broken.

✿ Expired poem

advice for dealing
with your toxic
parent
never raise your voice
first
they will don the
mask of victim
when they start shouting
at you
remember your ears
don't deserve this
noise
when they call you
a spoiled brat for
wanting food
remember you deserve
to eat
when they threaten
your security
remember you are always
welcome in our home

when she tries to steal
your joy
remember you have an
endless well within you
when they wish you
were never born
know that we thank God
for your existence
every day
when they forget
you are they're
child
remember we accept
you as our own
when she can't see you
for the wonder you are
remember we love you
always.

✤ **Blame**

where do you place
it?
and why?
is it with the
ears which choose
to listen
rather than close
it it with
the mind that
allows it to
absorb and be
convinced?
is it with the
soul that wishes
to be free
and is too much
of a coward
to flee?
is it the eyes
who look with
their gaze

instead of looking
away?
is it with the
feet which choose
to be glued
to the floor
refusing to move?
is it with the
heart which refuses
to stop feeling
and deceives your
senses?

❧ Drifting

Is your life
truly your own?
when you leave
everything to chance
the wind that blows
you from day to day
has more claim
on your life
than you do
the wind yearns for
a body
and you gave up
yours
how many hollow
bodies are out
there I wonder
playing host to
nothing
but wind.

❧ Comparing

After looking up
people from the
past
friends
girlfriends
classmates
seeing their life
progression and
choices
I can't help
but feel like
an escaped
mental patient
dithering away their
life in a
world all their own.

❧ A memento

You taught me
to be afraid
of women
to be afraid
to be touched
my fear will
be a constant
reminder of
you.

❧ The best you could do

After everything
was said and done
the best you
could come up
with was
"shit happens"
shit happened to
my face,
body,
and soul.

✤ Hotline

You made me
feel sorry for
you
when you told
me that you
couldn't get anyone
on the suicide
hot-line
that you started
cutting again
I can't forgive
you for that.

✿ Happy relationship

Nothing says happy
relationship better
than spilling something
on the futon
that is your bed
and feverishly trying
to clean it
up
 and trying to dry it
before your girlfriend
sees it
because you are
genuinely afraid of
her
and she deals out
corporal punishment.

Zipper

I'm very sorry
that I couldn't
zip up your
dress
obviously you are
the same size
it was my
fault
you had every
right to push
me into the
dresser
and threaten me
I don't deserve
to be with you.

❧ **Take your pills**

She was very
upset about
having to take
medication
all I was trying
to do was
give her the
anxiety pills
she reached up
and clawed my
face
we get into
an argument
this was how
most started
me upset how
she treated me
and her not
taking blame.

✧ The past

I feel like
things are starting
to come to a
head
all of the
old feelings from
the past are
resurfacing
and becoming a
solidified image
all that was unclear
is now gotten
a better pair of
glasses
it's a fresh wound
and old feelings
are made a new
the hurt is
fresh
the hate is
burning

and forgiveness is
far off
unattainable
unwanted
unsought
unwelcome
it's the solitude
of quarantine
a lone with our
thoughts
nothing to distract
they're untempered and
untethered
like a genie released
from imprisonment
pandora's box once
opened
whats unleashed cannot
be put back
it's grasping at
straws
air
nothing doing

living with the unleashed
is the only way
forward
a symbiotic relationship
co-dependance
cohabitation of one's
mind and demons
thats how you live
and survive with
the past.

✿ For example

Things you
taught me by
way of bad
example
I know that
after you
some things will
change
in future relationships
suspicion being
a big one
trusting my partner
not to cheat will
take work
right now it's
a given
learning not to
apply you to the
present is hard
learning the past
is not a good

example is hard
hoping that the
future will be
different than the
past
is hard
but necessary
knowing that not all
women are like you
is a relief
and a desperate
hope.

✤ Unlearning

Things to watch
out for in
future relationships
criticism is not
a personal attack
you know what that
sounds like
just because your
partner is mad
doesn't mean they
are going to hurt
you
you are used to
someone trying to
hurt your feelings
this one may not be
give them the benefit
of the doubt
you are used to
being on the
defensive

take a deep breath
and think
before reacting
your emotions may not
be right
your fear of your
partner is not
founded
they are not
the same person
the shadow of the
past
is on you
but it will
fade with time
monitor yourself
and pay attention
avoid triggers
and explain them when
unavoidable
and above all else
be kind to
yourself.

❧ Inner critic

In a way
she is still
with me
I only left her in
body
and proximity
she's still in
my head
her voice
her voice is very
clear
I hear her whenever
criticism is on
my mind
not any kind
for others
it's my voice
but for me
that voice is reserved
for her
I call her

my inner-critic
it's always been
there
lurking in the
recesses
but somehow I
listened more closely
and heard a familiar
voice
it was very unsettling
I thought I left
her behind
but a piece of her
managed to latch
itself
on me
or leave enough of
an impression to
stay permanent
for now
in this way
she still runs
my life

she tells me an
idea is stupid
any mistake I
make
any mess made
is a catastrophe
and the feeling of
impending doom
returns from the
grave of the
old relationship
to haunt me.

✖ Night Anthem

Feeling exhausted
my gut is acting
up again
haven't been sleeping
that well at all
stay up late at
night for some
reason
despite being completely
exhausted
why do I do it?
it's like an
addiction
force of habit
not staying up
is not an option
it wouldn't feel
right
being in bed at
a decent time
like wasting something

precious
with something as
dull as sleep.

❧ **Being Ugly**

Watching music videos
and interviews of
Dave Grohl
reflecting
on myself
comparing myself
wondering
why can't I be as
good looking as him
my hand reaches
the balding scalp
confirming what isn't
there
hasn't been for some
time
and never will
again
my beard is an
attempt to regain
some sense of confidence
self-worth

even
though it's starting
the betrayal like my
scalp before it
confirming my suspicion
on ugliness.

✥ **Your memory**

Trying to think
of things that
will make my
brain happy
my mind goes to
our summers on
Cape May
enjoying the victorian
haunted spooky town
the antique shops
spending all day
together
having adventures
enjoying life
I can't believe
I turned to your
memory
for serotonin.

❧ Existential dread

I am in a
constant state of
existential
dread
what is the point
of this
that
or anything else
looking before you
leap
taken to a higher
level of
fanaticism
loyal to the
well worn pattern
in the dirt road
of my everyday life
deviation unexplored
feared
and loathed
the path of routine

may be well worn
and comfortable
and it is all those
things
unapologetically so
it's there for you
like a beer is for
an alcoholic
only it comes with
less stigma
hell it's even
praised
your consistent
people know who you
are
what your about
what your gonna say
who your gonna do
and where
now that's marriage
material
but no
you can't think

of marriage
let alone describe
what it means
your too engrossed
by your own thoughts
the whys?
the hows?
the what fors?
you can't find
the meaning because
your not sure there is
any
your stuck in existential
dread
where there's no escape
from your
head.

✒ **Ode to typewriters**

Why use a
typewriter
when you can
type on the keys
of a computer
the words magically
appearing on the
screen
you'll just have
to retype it again
anyway to make it
digital
to send your email
manuscript
to the printers
it wouldn't be
the same
I'd miss the
concave polished
surface of the round
keys
cupping my finger tips

the clackity clack clack
of the violent hammer
strikes of words
on paper
making a poem
corporeal in this
world
making poetry on
a digital screen
is much like
making a painting
on a digital screen
sure it's faster
and cleaner
but it's not
real
it's imaginary
like the idea was
in the artist's head
only now it's stored in
a digital brain
my typewriter is like
a paintbrush

it brings ideas into
the real world.

❦ Infidelity

The only time
I think I
was capable of
taking a life
the most angry
and betrayed
one of the worst
drives of my life
was picking her up
from John's house
distractedly from her
mouth
unable to meet my
eyes
she confessed to
being raped
by the friend who
picked her up
earlier
everything turned red
I beet the steering wheel

with clenched fists
cursing his name
think of all the things
I could do
at home
she was calm
just like in the car
close friends called
pestering to help and
comfort
she wanted none
the nagging suspicions
crept through my mind
she did not want to
go to the E.R.
no testing
nothing
no crying
shock can act strangely
but stories told to
many
can unravel the falsehood
compared notes with others

and she unraveled
the rescuer with brandished
knife
was himself a coward
and not involved
the accused was in
possession of telling texts
and photos
she arranged the events
and had sexted him many
days before
the "victim" was really
the accused
whose only crime was
being mislead
why'd she do it
we all wondered
what was there to gain?
perhaps she felt
guilt for cheating
on me
and it was the only
way she could cope

though it wan't her
first dance with
infidelity
no
I think she enjoyed
seeing me squirm
hurt
feel empowered by her
control of my feelings
she said it once
years ago
she pretended to be
pregnant
just for a moment
when I recouped
and asked her why
she said
"I just wanted
to see your reaction."

Email
cafeconfessionalbook@gmail.com
for more information,